CELEBRITY BIOS

LeAnn Rimes

Kristin McCracken

Children's Press
A Division of Scholastic Inc.
New York / Toronto / London / Auckland / Sydney
Mexico City / New Delhi / Hong Kong
Danbury, Connecticut

To Tanessa: Twang on!

Contributing Editor: Jennifer Ceaser
Book Design: Nelson Sa

Photo Credits: Cover, pp. 4, 6, 9, 11 © Everett Collection; p. 13 © Fitzroy Barrett/Globe Photos Inc.; pp. 15, 16, 18 © Everett Collection; p. 20 © Sonia Moskowitz/Globe Photos Inc.; p. 21 © Fitzroy Barrett/Globe Photos Inc; p. 23 © Everett Collection; p. 24 © Everett Collection; p. 27 © Fitzroy Barrett/Globe Photos Inc; p. 30 © Andrea Renault/Globe Photos Inc; p. 33 © Andrea Renault/Globe Photos Inc; p. 35 © Lisa Rose/Globe Photos Inc; p. 36 © Fitzroy Barrett/Globe Photos Inc.

Library of Congress Cataloging-in-Publication Data

McCracken, Kristin.
    LeAnn Rimes / by Kristin McCracken.
      p. cm. (Celebrity bios)
    Includes bibliographical references and index.
    ISBN 0-516-23419-6 (lib. bdg.)–ISBN 0-516-23581-8 (pbk.)
      1. Rimes, LeAnn—Juvenile literature. 2. Country musicians—United States—Biography—Juvenile literature [1. Rimes, LeAnn. 2. Musicians. 3. Women—Biography. 4. Country music.] I. Title. II. Series.

ML3930.R56 M35 2000
782.421642'092—dc21
[B]
                                                              00-031671

CONTENTS

CHAPTER ONE

THE EARLY YEARS

"If you have a dream or goal, don't stop until you reach it. If you really want to accomplish something, don't let anyone stand in your way."

—LeAnn in the biography
LeAnn Rimes: Teen Country Queen

By the time LeAnn Rimes turned eighteen in August 2000, she had been a celebrity for more than five years. She has achieved worldwide fame and has received many awards for her hit songs and sold-out performances. She's also cowritten a novel and has starred in the TV movie made from the book.

LeAnn Rimes is just a teenager, but she's been performing for many years.

LeAnn Rimes and her parents are very close.

These are not the accomplishments of a typical American teenager. But this talented young singer is hardly a typical teenager.

YOUNG LeANN

On August 28, 1982, Margaret LeAnn Rimes was born to Wilbur and Belinda Rimes in

Jackson, Mississippi. Her parents were high-school sweethearts who lived in Flowood, a small suburb of Jackson, Mississippi.

Music came naturally to LeAnn. Her parents both loved to sing, and her father played guitar. In one biography, LeAnn described herself at two years old: "I could sing better than I could talk. You could understand every word when I was singing. But you couldn't understand what I was saying when I talked." Wilbur Rimes immediately recognized his young daughter's talents. He recorded LeAnn singing songs such as "You Are My Sunshine" and songs from Broadway musicals. LeAnn could even yodel!

LeAnn also loved to dance and took many lessons when she was a child. When LeAnn was four, her dance teacher suggested that she try out for a talent show. LeAnn's parents thought she was too young. They waited a year until they thought she was ready. At age five, LeAnn entered a local talent show. She performed "Getting to Know You," from the musical *The King and I*. LeAnn won first place!

OFF TO TEXAS

After her impressive debut, LeAnn knew that she wanted to be an entertainer. Her parents knew their daughter had talent. So in 1988, they decided to move to Garland, Texas, which is near Dallas. In Dallas, LeAnn would have more chances to develop her talents.

Soon after she settled in Texas, LeAnn tried out for a role in the Broadway production of *Annie II*, the sequel to the musical *Annie*. LeAnn didn't get the part. She was very disappointed, but her parents told her to keep her chin up. "It was difficult when I lost the role," LeAnn admitted in her biography. "But my parents were great. They were really there

LeAnn always wanted to be an entertainer.

for me. Now I look back on that time as a learning experience."

LeAnn had better luck the next year. She was just seven years old when she was chosen to play Tiny Tim in a Dallas production of *A Christmas Carol.* LeAnn had a great time, and the critics loved her performance.

In 1989 and 1990, LeAnn sang at many other events in Texas, including rodeos and

county fairs. She also began performing regularly at the Johnnie High Country Music Revue. People came from miles around to hear the young girl sing classic country songs.

A RISING STAR

In 1991, when LeAnn was eight, she got another big break. She was chosen to sing on a national television show called "Star Search." The way "Star Search" works is that each week, two singers in each age group compete. The judges pick a winner. The winner comes back the following week to defend his or her title. LeAnn won, and then she came back the next week and won again. She lost in her third week, but she was not discouraged. After LeAnn had had a taste of national television, she wanted more!

LeAnn went back to Dallas more determined than ever to become a star. She continued to sing at local shows for the next

LeAnn got her start performing at local rodeos and fairs in Texas.

two years. Her voice kept getting stronger with practice. She was ready for the big time.

OUT OF THE BLUE

In 1993, LeAnn met Bill Mack, a local disc jockey in Dallas. Mack had met LeAnn's singing idol, Patsy Cline, back in the 1950s.

Mack had even written a song for Cline. Unfortunately, Cline died before she had the chance to record it. That song was "Blue."

When Bill Mack heard LeAnn sing, she was just ten years old. He was amazed at how much she sounded like Patsy Cline. He knew that if LeAnn could sing "Blue," it would become a big hit.

Mack sent LeAnn a tape of the song. When LeAnn and her father were picking songs for an album they hoped to record, LeAnn decided to record "Blue."

SHE'S ALL THAT

LeAnn did not yet have a contract with one of the big record companies. She and her father had to find people who were willing to invest money in her talents. These investors paid for LeAnn to record her first CD in 1993. The CD was called *All That* and was released by Nor Va Jak, a small record label.

LeAnn's voice often is compared to that of the 1950s country-music star Patsy Cline.

At first, LeAnn sold *All That* to the fans who came to her performances in Dallas. Soon, Blockbuster Music began to sell the CD at their stores. People outside of Mississippi and Texas began hearing about the little blonde with the huge voice.

LeAnn loved to sing, but her talent didn't make her popular with her schoolmates. She told E!Online: "If I did something around

Dallas, the principal might post a story if it was in the newspaper. It got to the point where some people used to hate it . . . I really got picked on a lot." So, instead of going to school, LeAnn studied at home with a private tutor. The tutor was so impressed with LeAnn's academic abilities that LeAnn skipped two grades.

SIGNING A CONTRACT

After two years of trying to get the best record contract for LeAnn, Wilbur Rimes finally found the record label for which he wanted his daughter to work. Curb Records was known for turning young, unknown performers into superstars. The minute the label's owner, Mike Curb, heard LeAnn sing, he knew that he had found his next project. LeAnn signed a contract with Curb in the spring of 1995.

LeAnn worked in the studio for the next year. She rerecorded the song "Blue." The rest of the songs were a mixture of the new

LeAnn not only sings but also writes music.

country sound and older, more traditional country music. LeAnn had been writing songs, too. She recorded one of the songs that she cowrote, "Talk to Me."

CHAPTER TWO

BREAKING OUT

Looking out into the great unknown
I can feel my heart beating faster as I step out
on my own
There's a new horizon and the promise of favorable wind
I'm heading out tonight, traveling light . . .
            —"One Way Ticket (Because I Can)"
from the album *Blue*

In early 1996, when LeAnn was just thirteen years old, Curb Records began to spread the word about the young star. The album wasn't yet ready, but the record company released copies of four songs to radio stations. One of the songs was "Blue." When radio stations began to play the song, listeners loved it. They called their local radio stations to find out

LeAnn's first hit song was "Blue."

more about LeAnn. They wanted to hear the song over and over again.

By the summer of 1996, "Blue" had risen to number ten on the Billboard country chart. When the single was released in June, "Blue" quickly became the most popular country song in the United States. For twenty weeks in a row, "Blue" was the number-one country hit in the nation. An *Entertainment Weekly* review of the song claimed that LeAnn "has got a voice that'll just knock you out. She's gonna go right to the top."

LISTENERS LOVE LeANN

While the song "Blue" was climbing up the charts, LeAnn was putting the finishing touches on her album, also called *Blue. Blue* landed in stores on July 9, 1996. It didn't stay on the shelves for long. *Blue* became the best-selling country album in the United States in its very first week. Country music fans

In 1996, LeAnn's album *Blue* hit number one.

weren't the only ones buying the CD. Fans of other types of music liked LeAnn Rimes, too. *Blue* rose as high as number four on the Billboard 200 Album chart.

Later on that year, Curb Records released the single "One Way Ticket (Because I Can)." It became LeAnn's second number-one country single. Meanwhile, *Blue* was the number-one country music album in the nation. This made LeAnn one of the youngest performers to have both the most popular song and album at the same time! By August, when LeAnn turned fourteen, more than 800,000 copies of *Blue* had been sold. (As of April 2000, *Blue* had gone multiplatinum, selling eight million copies.)

In 1997, LeAnn won two Grammy Awards.

AWARD WINNER

In the fall of 1996, LeAnn was nominated for two Country Music Awards. One was the Horizon Award for Best New Artist and the other was for Song of the Year (for "Blue"). The night of the awards show was one of the highlights of LeAnn's year. The show was held at the Grand Ole Opry, a famous music hall in Nashville. Although LeAnn didn't win either award for which she was nominated, she was asked to open the show by singing the song "Blue."

In early 1997, LeAnn was nominated for four Grammy Awards, the music industry's biggest honor. She won two of the awards: Best New Artist and Best Female Country Vocal. At the Billboard Music Awards,

LeAnn holds one of her Billboard Music Awards.

LeAnn won three awards: Artist of the Year, Country Artist of the Year, and Country Album of the Year for *Blue*. She also won an American Music Award for Best New Country Artist.

A LITTLE OLD, A LITTLE NEW

Many fans had never heard of LeAnn Rimes before 1996, so they never got the chance to buy her first record, *All That*. LeAnn decided to rerecord some of that album's songs for her fans. She also recorded a hit song from the 1960s, "Unchained Melody." The result was the album *Unchained Melody: The Early Years*. It was released in February of 1997.

In May, LeAnn released a new single called "How Do I Live?" The song was featured on the soundtrack to the movie *Con Air*. That summer, it seemed as though every radio station in the country was playing LeAnn's smash hit. "How Do I Live?" set a record by staying on the Billboard singles chart for sixty-nine weeks in a row.

LeAnn then decided to record cover songs (remakes of older songs). The album, *You Light Up My Life: Inspirational Songs,* was released in September 1997. The album included some of LeAnn's favorite songs, including "You Light Up My Life," the classic hymn "Amazing Grace," and "The Star Spangled Banner." The album also featured the hit song "How Do I Live?"

How well did this album sell? It became the biggest-selling album in the country in its very first week. It became country music's best-selling record, with four million copies sold. LeAnn was not just a country sensation anymore. She had become a music superstar.

LeAnn is one of country music's best-selling artists.

Even with all of her success, LeAnn kept looking ahead. "I've established my singing career, and I want to maintain it," she told E!Online, "but I also want to build up something else."

So what would be next for the talented Miss Rimes?

CHAPTER THREE

TOP OF THE WORLD

"I'd like to mix it up a little bit and broaden everything. I'm just kind of growing and pushing the limits and seeing what people will let me do and what I can do."
—**LeAnn in an interview with *E!Online***

In addition to releasing two albums in 1997, LeAnn developed her talents in other ways. She wrote a book called *Holiday In Your Heart*. LeAnn's book was part autobiography, part fiction. It told the story of Anna Lee, a teenage country singer. Anna Lee was faced with the choice of singing at the Grand Ole Opry or spending time with her sick

LeAnn is both a successful singer and actress.

grandmother at home in Mississippi. Because the story took place at Christmastime, the publishing company released the book in November, hoping it would be a great holiday gift. The book went on to sell 100,000 copies.

The ABC television network also was interested in LeAnn's story. The network decided to make a TV movie of the book. They asked LeAnn to star in it. LeAnn had not done any real acting (other than in music videos) since she was eight years old. However, she was confident in her acting abilities. LeAnn recalled in E!Online that the role "was kind of easy for me to do because the character basically was me, but in a different way." Many of LeAnn's fans tuned in to see *Holiday In Your Heart* in December of 1997.

A NEW ROLE, A NEW ALBUM

LeAnn enjoyed acting in the TV movie. So she was delighted when she was asked in early

LeAnn starred in the TV movie *Holiday in Your Heart.*

1998 to appear on her favorite soap opera, "Days of Our Lives." LeAnn played a runaway teen named Madison. The character did not appear in many episodes, but it was a satisfying role for LeAnn.

Did you know?

When LeAnn tours, she takes a bus. But it isn't just any old bus—it's a private bus with beds, a kitchen, and entertainment equipment. She tours with her band, her parents, and her tutor.

LeAnn also went back to the studio in 1998 to record her fourth album for Curb Records. *Sittin' on Top of the World* was released in May of that year. The album's catchy tunes included the hits "Committed" and "Looking Through Your Eyes," which was featured on the soundtrack for the animated film *Quest for Camelot*. However, the style of the songs on *Sittin' on Top of the World* was pop, not country. The songs did not appeal to many of LeAnn's country fans. LeAnn explained to Country Weekly Online: "I love country music and will never turn my back on country music. But I also enjoy singing other styles of music."

SWEET SIXTEEN

In the summer of 1998, LeAnn joined country singer Bryan White on a nationwide concert tour called Something to Talk About. The two young stars had a great time. But LeAnn was exhausted by the end of the year. She had been touring for three years without a break. She wanted to spend some time relaxing at home with her family and friends. LeAnn explained to Country Weekly Online: "Life on the road does get very tiring. You're on a schedule all the time and you're trying to please a lot of people. It's a tough part of the business."

LeAnn turned sixteen in August of that year. In Country Weekly Online, she joked, "They won't be able to call me a fifteen-year-old singing sensation any more. I guess they'll call me a sixteen-year-old singing sensation."

After her tour finished at the end of the year, LeAnn and her mother decided to move to Los Angeles. There, LeAnn could take acting lessons, go to auditions, perform on television shows, or just relax in the California sunshine.

IN THE SPOTLIGHT

In 1999, LeAnn did some more television work. She was a guest star on teen star Brandy's TV show, "Moesha." She also acted as the celebrity host for the American Music Awards. In April 1999, LeAnn was asked to

perform on VH1's "Divas Live '99" show. This was a great honor for LeAnn. She got to perform with famous singers such as Whitney Houston, Tina Turner, Cher, Brandy, Mary J. Blige, and Faith Hill.

Later that year, Country Music Television (CMT) featured a special on LeAnn. "CMT All Access: LeAnn Rimes" premiered in October. It aired several times during the next few months.

LeAnn is definitely still interested in trying her luck as an actress, but she's in no hurry. What kind of film would she want to do? "I'd like to do something that deals with real life—about real life and young adults," she told Country Weekly Online. "A love story, maybe."

BACK TO COUNTRY

Even though 1999 was supposed to be a year of rest, LeAnn couldn't leave music too far behind. She recorded the song "Leaving's Not

LeAnn performed on the VH1 special "Divas Live '99."

Leaving" for the soundtrack to the film *Anywhere But Here,* starring Natalie Portman. LeAnn also went back into the studio. She decided to go back to her roots and cut an album of country songs. It included six songs made famous by her idol, Patsy Cline. These included the songs "Crazy" and "I Fall to Pieces."

The album, simply titled *LeAnn Rimes,* was the seventeen-year-old singer's fifth album. It was released in October 1999. The record's old-time sound brought back LeAnn's original country fans. "I've had so many people ask me to do an album of country's more traditional songs. And I've wanted to do one because I love traditional country music," she explained in Country Weekly Online. The record also featured a new hit single, "Big Deal."

LeAnn Rimes was different for LeAnn because she had more of a say in the way the record was made. "In the past, I didn't want to

In late 1999, LeAnn released her fifth album, which featured traditional country music.

be involved. Now, I put a lot of thought into what goes into each cut to make it the best it can be," LeAnn explained in her biography.

BRANCHING OUT

As LeAnn left the 1990s behind, she looked ahead to new interests. In 2000, LeAnn joined forces with artists such as Hootie and the Blowfish and Tracy Chapman to create a soundtrack for the TV miniseries *Jesus*. The show, which aired in May, featured songs by new singers in an effort to appeal to young viewers. LeAnn recorded the song "I Believe in You" for the miniseries. Her song played during the show's closing credits.

LeAnn also had the honor of performing a duet with Elton John, called "Written In The Stars." She performed the song on TV for the "People's Choice Awards," "Late Night with David Letterman," and the "Today Show." LeAnn told Country Weekly Online of her great experience working with Elton John: "He's so nice and funny and completely down-to-earth. We instantly became friends."

LeAnn and her boyfriend Andrew Keegan cohosted the TV show "Class of 2000."

In April 2000, LeAnn was in Nashville to tape the new TNN show "Class of 2000." LeAnn's boyfriend, Andrew Keegan (from "Party of Five"), cohosted the show with her. The show helps new young singers and dancers to get noticed.

CHAPTER FOUR

FACING THE FUTURE WITH STYLE

"I'd say in the last year and a half I've come into my own style. I'd call it fun, sexy, and sleek."

—LeAnn in *InStyle*

LeAnn has grown up a lot since she won her first Grammy Award at age fourteen. Now a young woman, LeAnn has adopted a new, stylish look. As every girl does, LeAnn mixes her styles to match her different moods. She loves to wear leather during the daytime, and counts her Christina Perrin pants, a Henry Duarte

LeAnn shows off her new stylish look at a party for *Vanity Fair* magazine.

jacket, and Harley Davidson boots among her favorite items. For nighttime glamour, she may step out wearing fashions from Gucci, Chloé, or Dolce & Gabbana. She also wears her favorite item every day—a Cartier watch.

LeAnn keeps trim by kickboxing and lifting weights every day with her personal trainer. She also stays on a healthy diet. "I watch what I eat, but I eat what I want," LeAnn told *InStyle.* "I never deprive myself."

LeAnn likes the new line of Calvin Klein makeup, but she doesn't like to look made-up. "I like being a normal person, being able to walk out of the house without makeup on," LeAnn explained to *InStyle.*

WHAT'S NEXT?

What's in store for LeAnn Rimes? On her next album, LeAnn is excited to try something new. "Next time, I'm going to totally come back with something no one's ever heard from me before . . . something a little alternative," she revealed to the *London Times.* "I'd say it lies somewhere between Alanis and Jewel. It's a direction I've wanted to take for a long time now."

Other than her music, LeAnn's interest in trying new things makes it hard to predict her future. LeAnn might pursue a full-time acting career. She may head to Broadway to perform in musicals. Someday, she may even go to college. "I've always wanted to help children, and I've thought about studying speech pathology," LeAnn told Country.com.

Whatever LeAnn pursues, she is sure to be a success. "I still have more dreams," she confessed to Country Weekly Online. "And I'm ready to make those dreams come true." She added, "The little girl has grown up. I am a new LeAnn . . . I feel like I'm ready to take on a whole new world."

TIMELINE

1982 •LeAnn Rimes is born in Jackson, Mississippi, on August 28.

1987 •LeAnn wins her first talent show at age five.

1998 •The Rimes family moves to Garland, Texas.
      •LeAnn begins performing in the Dallas area.

1991 •LeAnn is a two-week champion on "Star Search."

1993 •With her father, LeAnn records her first CD, *All That.*

1996 •LeAnn's major-label debut, *Blue,* is released.
      •LeAnn's first single, "Blue," sky-rockets to the top of the charts.
      •The album *Blue* debuts at number one on the Billboard country chart.
      •LeAnn performs at the Grand Ole Opry in September.

1996
- LeAnn is nominated for Country Music Awards (CMA) for Best New Artist and Song of the Year.

1997
- LeAnn releases *Unchained Melody: The Early Years* in February.
- LeAnn's book *Holiday in Your Heart* is published.
- In December, LeAnn stars in the TV movie of *Holiday in Your Heart* on ABC.
- LeAnn's parents divorce.
- LeAnn wins an American Music Award for Best New Country Artist.
- LeAnn wins two Grammy Awards: Best New Artist and Best Female Country Vocal.
- LeAnn wins three Billboard Music Awards: Artist of the Year, Country Artist of the Year, and Country Album of the Year.
- *You Light up My Life: Inspirational Songs* hits record stores in September.

TIMELINE

1998
- LeAnn guest stars on the soap opera "Days of Our Lives."
- *Sittin' On Top of the World* is released in May.
- LeAnn tours with Bryan White.
- LeAnn and her mother move to California.

1999
- LeAnn sings "Leaving's Not Leaving" for the soundtrack to the film *Anywhere But Here.*
- LeAnn guest stars on "Moesha."
- LeAnn performs on "Divas Live '99" in April.
- *LeAnn Rimes* is released in October.

2000
- LeAnn records and performs a duet with Elton John.
- LeAnn is named one of *Teen People*'s "Hot 21 Under 21."

2001
- *God Bless America* and *I Need You* are released.

2002
- *Twisted Angel* is released.

FACT SHEET

Name	Margaret LeAnn Rimes
Birthdate	August 28, 1982
Birthplace	Jackson, Mississippi
Family	Wilbur and Belinda, divorced; no siblings
Hometown	Dallas, Texas (Garland)
Sign	Virgo
Hair/Eyes	Blonde/Blue
Height	5' 5"
Pet	Shakes, a Jack Russell Terrier
Cars	BMW 840, Range Rover (SUV)

Favorites

Actors	Mel Gibson, Robin Williams, Morgan Freeman, Kevin Costner
Actresses	Jodie Foster, Whoopi Goldberg
Movies	*The Shawshank Redemption, Twister, The Bodyguard*
TV Shows	"Friends," "Beverly Hills 90210," "Days of Our Lives"
Foods	Cheese crackers, pizza, chicken, steak, potatoes
Drink	strawberry ice cream soda
Colors	red, black
Musicians	Elton John, Madonna, Reba McEntire, Prince, Barbra Streisand
Hobbies	horseback riding, kickboxing

NEW WORDS

audition a tryout for a movie, TV show, or play

autobiography a book that a person writes about his or her own life

Broadway a section of New York City where theaters present dramas and musicals

chart a listing that ranks music sales

debut a performer's first appearance

duet a song featuring vocals by two singers

Grammy an award given in recognition of musical achievement

hymn song sung in praise of God

independent label small record company that usually only distributes albums to local stores

kickboxing a form of self-defense that combines rapid kicking movements with boxing moves

miniseries a television movie that runs for two or more days

multiplatinum a record that sells more than one million copies

musical a play with singing and dancing

nominated chosen for an award

novel a book that tells a fictional (made-up) story

producer the person who supervises and finances the production of a record, film, or television program

recording studio place where a record is recorded and produced

revue a music concert which features many performers, often held outside at fairgrounds

role the part an actor or actress plays in a movie or TV show

sequel follow-up to a movie

soap opera a television drama that airs in continuous episodes

soundtrack an album of songs that are connected to a movie, TV show, or play

FOR FURTHER READING

Bego, Mark. *LeAnn Rimes*. New York: Saint Martin's Press, 1998.

Britton, Tamara L. and Lori K. Pupeza. *LeAnn Rimes*. Minneapolis, MN: ABDO Publishing Company, 1999.

Catalano, Grace. *LeAnn Rimes: Teen Country Queen*. New York: Bantam Doubleday Dell Books for Young Readers, 1997.

Sgammato, Joe. *Dream Come True: The LeAnn Rimes Story*. New York: Ballantine Books, 1997.

Zymet, Cathy A. *LeAnn Rimes*. Broomall, PA: Chelsea House Publishers, 1999.

RESOURCES

Billboard Online
www.billboard.com
This site offers information about all your favorite singers, including LeAnn. See how her records and singles are doing on the charts and read the latest news about LeAnn.

Country Weekly Online
www.countryweekly.com
This online magazine provides all the latest news about your favorite country stars, including LeAnn!

Independent Movie Database
www.imdb.com/Name?Rimes,+LeAnn
This site lists LeAnn's acting credits and upcoming projects. There also is a brief biography and interesting trivia.

Rimes Times
www.rimestimes.com
At LeAnn's official Web site, you can join her fan club, find out the latest concert information, and read letters written by LeAnn.

INDEX

About the Author

Kristin McCracken is an educator and writer living in New York City. Her favorite activities include seeing movies, plays, and the occasional star on the street.